Little Kalidasas' Samskritam

K-Group (skanda-gaNapatI)

By Srikali Goutam Varanasi-Vedanthi

A Little Kalidasas' Publication
San Leandro, CA, USA

Little Kalidasas' Samskritam K-Group (skanda-gaNapatI)
By Srikali Goutam Varanasi-Vedanthi

Little Kalidasas' Publications
576 Thornton Street, San Leandro, CA - 94577
Find us at: www.littlekalidasas.org

First Edition: 2015

ISBN: 978-1-312-85880-0

Edited by Sudhindra Goutam Vedanthi
Reviewed and Proof Read by Srivishnu Goutam Vedanthi
Logo design by Sumedh Goutam Vedanthi

This edition is published by Little Kalidasas with permission from Simple
Learnings Series. The Simple Learnings Series is a creator of educational learning tools.

Little Kalidasas is a nonprofit organization, with a mission to provide creative
learning methods for all, with an aim to nurture learners, to lead lives in better
ways with added values and to serve for the greater good of humanity. Little
Kalidasas teachings include creativity, wisdom, compassion, forgiveness and
service.

Dedication

To the supreme god shrimAnnArAyaNa (श्रीमन्नारायणाय)

Acknowledgement

Bringing this book to the print would not have been possible without the enthusiasm of all the wonderful children, and adults who were passionate about learning Samskritam. Thanks to each and every one of them. I am indebted to my Gurus, my parents, my parents-in-law and mentors for their blessings in this great journey. I thank my children for bringing more joy and pleasure throughout this process, and to my husband for being the backbone for this entire effort.

Table of Contents

Introduction

This book is written by the creative contributors of Little Kalidasas, a non-profit organization with an aim to work with kids, teens, parents, adults and grandparents. The main purpose is to bring the joy and bliss of learning, sharing, and serving. During this learning process everyone will experience the strength in teaming and togetherness.

This learning aid is developed with an aim to teach Samskritam to children between ages 3 to 6 years and to starters of all ages without any Sanskrit background.

This book contains 10 lessons. Each lesson consists of some writing, speaking, vocabulary, and worksheets to practice. Five aspects of learning are emphasized, viz., chanting, listening, speaking, writing, and reading. Kids in this group enjoy learning lessons with lots of creative rhymes and sing-along songs.

Learning Objectives

1. Prayer Shlokas (Three shlokas - gaNesha, sarasvatI and guru)

2. Vowels (अ to अः) – devanAgari and transliteration

3. Rhymes (vowel, numbers, animals, birds, fruits, मम नाम, body parts)

4. Picture Stories, e.g. Thirsty Crow Story

5. shrugAla Musical (Shorter version)

6. rAma shabda (chanting only, memorization not required)

7. mangaLa shloka and shAnti mantra

8. Vocabulary - Numbers 1-12/ Animals / Fruits / Vegetables/ Body Parts/ Birds

9. Other Learning Items – hariH Om, namaste, dhanyavAdaH,

10. Amruta Bhashanam (मम नाम, मम पिता, मम माता, मम मित्रम्, मम with vocab words, भवतः नाम किम्, भवत्याः नाम किम्)

11. bhAratIya samskRutiH- Indian Culture– Hindu Gods

12. Activities – Coloring of Gods' pictures etc.

13. Project – poster, collage etc.

14. Course Evaluation

।। प्रार्थना श्लोकाः ।।

(prArthanA shlokAH)

वक्रतुण्ड महाकाय सुर्यकोटिसमप्रभ।

निर्विघ्नं कुरु मे देव सर्वकार्येषु सर्वदा॥

vakratuNDa mahAkAya suryakoTisamaprabha ।

nirvighnaM kuru me deva sarvakaaryeShu sarvadaa ॥

सरस्वति नमस्तुभ्यं वरदे कामरूपिणि ।

विद्यारम्भं करिष्यामि सिद्धिर्भवतु मे सदा ॥

sarasvati namastubhyaM varade kAmarUpiNi ।

vidyArambhaM kariShyAmi siddhirbhavatu me sadA ॥

गुरुर्ब्रह्मा गुरुर्विष्णुः गुरुर्देवो महेश्वरः ।

गुरुस्साक्षात् परब्रह्म तस्मै श्री गुरवे नमः ॥

gururbrahmA gururviShNuH gururdevo maheshvaraH ।

gurussAkShAt parabrahma tasmai shrI gurave namaH ॥

Peace Mantras

॥ मङ्गळ श्लोकः ॥

|| mangaLa shlokaH ||

पुरे ग्रामे गृहे कुट्यां बालो वृद्धो युवापि च।

करोतु संस्कृताभ्यासं प्राप्नोतु सुखसम्पदम् ॥

pure grAme gRuhe kuTyaaM baalo vRuddho yuvApi cha |

karotu saMskRutAbhyAsaM prApnotu sukhasampadam ||

॥ शान्ति-मन्त्रः ॥

|| shaanti-mantraH ||

ॐ शान्तिः शान्तिः शान्तिः ॥

oum shAntiH shAntiH shAntiH ||

शब्द-अनुवदनम् - _shabda chanting_

अकारान्तः पुंलिङ्गः "राम" शब्दः		
रामः	रामौ	रामाः
हे राम	हे रामौ	हे रामाः
रामम्	रामौ	रामान्
रामेण	रामाभ्याम्	रामैः
रामाय	रामाभ्याम्	रामेभ्यः
रामात्	रामाभ्याम्	रामेभ्यः
रामस्य	रामयोः	रामाणाम्
रामे	रामयोः	रामेषु

akArAntaH puMli~ggaH "rAma" shabdaH		
rAmaH	rAmau	rAmAH
he rAma	he rAmau	he rAmAH
rAmam	rAmau	rAmAn
rAmeNa	rAmAbhyAm	rAmaiH
rAmAya	rAmAbhyAm	rAmebhyaH
rAmAt	rAmAbhyAm	rAmebhyaH
rAmasya	rAmayOH	rAmANAm
rAme	rAmayOH	rAmeShu

Lesson 1 – प्रथमः पाठः

In this lesson you will learn to start writing in Sanskrit. Sanskrit script is called *'devanAgari'*, which means God's language. We will also introduce you to writing Sanskrit in English like language. This process is called ***transliteration***.

Sanskrit is rightly referred to as "*samskRutam*". We will be learning the Sanskrit alphabet starting with the vowels in this level. Without any delay, let's learn the Sanskrit Alphabet.

 Writing

Sanskrit Alphabet	Transliteration	Pronunciation Guide
अ	a	h<u>u</u>t
आ	aa or A	f<u>a</u>ther

Pronunciation in Sanskrit is very simple. Especially, vowels need the least amount of effort. All vowels pronounced by opening your mouth without any obstruction. Practice with the help of a *Guru,* to write and pronounce these two vowels correctly. There are three worksheets given after this first lesson. Practice them well. Good handwriting is a basis for great learning. Also, when you write nicely, Sanskrit letters get extra beauty.

 अमृतभाषणम् – amRutabhAShaNam – Spoken Exercises

In this section, we will introduce you to spoken Sanskrit exercises.

Exercise 1: To introduce yourself and tell your name:

मम नाम _____ । (mama nAma _____)

Fill in the blank with your name. Example:

मम नाम श्रीकाली (mama nAma shrikAll)

Note: Contents in this section can be remembered by using rhymes taught by your teacher in the class.

शब्दकोशः - shabdakoshaH - Vocabulary Words

 गजः (gajaH)

 सिंहः (simhaH)

 सर्पः (sarpaH)

 शशः (shashaH)

1. Follow the rhyme from the teacher and memorize the words and their meanings.

2. Exercise: Make up your own tune, using the words above.

भारतीयसंस्कृतिः – Indian Culture

In this section, you will be learning about Hindu Gods. For the activities related to this section you will either color the given coloring sheet or draw on your own.

In this first lesson, your teacher will teach you about the Hindu God "*gaNesha*" (Ganesha).

Name: _____   **Date**: _____

अ   अ   अ   अ   अ   अ   अ

अ   अ   अ   अ   अ   अ   अ

Name: _____   **Date**: _____

आ   आ   आ   आ   आ   आ

आ   आ   आ   आ   आ   आ

Name: _____   **Date:** _____

अ आ   अ आ   अ आ

अ आ   अ आ   अ आ

Lesson 2 – द्वितीयः पाठः

In this lesson, you will learn the next two vowels. Hope you have already practiced writing the first two vowels अ and आ.   Do not forget: Learning is cumulative. Whatever you have learned in the previous class is going to be crucial for further progression.

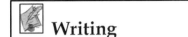 **Writing**

Sanskrit Alphabet	Transliteration	Pronunciation Guide
इ	i	s<u>i</u>t
ई	I	sw<u>ee</u>t

Recall - In samskRutam, pronunciation is simple and important. All vowels are pronounced by opening your mouth without any obstruction. Practice with the help of a *Guru*. There are three worksheets given after this lesson. Practice them well. A short vowel uses one unit of time and a long vowel uses two units of time.

 अमृतभाषणम् – amRutabhAShaNam – Spoken Exercises

In the last lesson, you have learned how to tell your name and introduce yourself. Review it.

Exercise 1: To introduce yourself and tell your name:

मम नाम _____ । (mama nAma _____)

Fill in the blank with your name. Example:

मम नाम श्रीकाली (mama nAma shrikAlI)

Exercise 2: There is another way to introduce yourself and tell your name.

अहं _____ ।

(aham _____ ।)

> Fill in the blank with your name. Example:
>
> अहं गौतमः ।   (aham gautamaH ।)

शब्दकोशः - shabdakoshaH - Vocabulary Words

 एकम् (ekam)

 द्वे (dve)

 त्रीणि (trINi)

 चत्वारि (chatvAri)

 पञ्च (pa~jcha)

 षट् (ShuT)

(pronounce as "pancha")

1. Follow the rhyme from the teacher and memorize the numbers.

2. Exercise: Practice telling the numbers from 1 to 6 and in the reverse order from 6 to 1. Also try recalling any number randomly.

भारतीयसंस्कृतिः – Indian Culture

Remember, in this section, you will be learning about Hindu Gods.

In this lesson your teacher will teach you about the Hindu God "*skanda*" also known as "*kArtikeya*".

Name: _____   Date: _____

इ   इ   इ   इ   इ   इ   इ

इ   इ   इ   इ   इ   इ   इ

Name: _____   **Date:** _____

ई ई ई ई ई ई ई

ई ई ई ई ई ई ई

Name: _____   **Date:** _____

इ   ई   इ   ई   इ   ई   इ   ई

इ   ई   इ   ई   इ   ई   इ   ई

Lesson 3 – तृतीयः पाठः

In this lesson, you will learn the next two vowels. Hope you have already practiced writing the first four vowels अ, आ, इ, ई. {**Do not forget:** Learning is cumulative. Whatever you have learned in the previous class is important for further progression}.

 Writing

Sanskrit Alphabet	Transliteration	Pronunciation Guide
उ	u	p<u>u</u>t
ऊ	U	m<u>oo</u>n

Note: Not all sounds have an exact English word.

 अमृतभाषणम् – amRutabhAShaNam – Spoken Exercises

In the last lesson, you have learned how to tell your name and introduce yourself in two ways.

Review it. Now we will see how to say Hello, and Thank you.

Exercise 1: How do we greet someone in Sanskrit?

1. हरिः ॐ (hariH Om) 2. नमस्ते । (namaste.)

> **Remember:** namaste and hariH Om does not translate exactly as 'Hello'. They are just equivalents and differ in elegance.

Exercise 2: How to say 'Thank You'. => धन्यवादः (dhanyavAdaH)

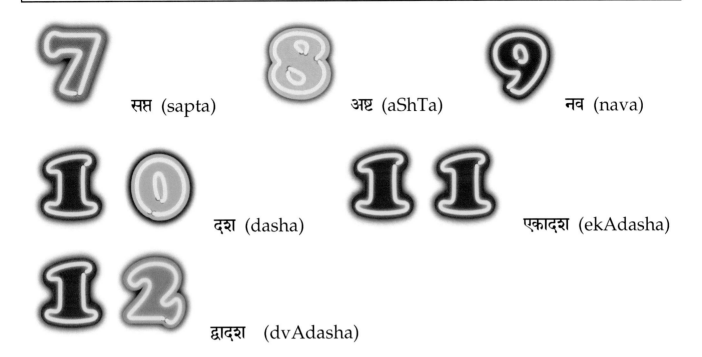

सप्त (sapta)   अष्ट (aShTa)   नव (nava)

दश (dasha)   एकादश (ekAdasha)

द्वादश (dvAdasha)

1. Follow the rhyme from the teacher and memorize the numbers.

2. Exercise: Practice telling the numbers from 1 to 12 and in the reverse order from 12 to 1. Also try recalling any number randomly.

भारतीयसंस्कृतिः – Indian Culture

In this lesson, your teacher will teach you about the Hindu God "*shiva*". Complete the activities following your teacher's suggestions. Coloring activity increases your sense of understanding and also gives happiness.

Name: _____   **Date:** _____

उ   उ   उ   उ   उ   उ   उ

उ   उ   उ   उ   उ   उ   उ

Name: _____   **Date:** _____

ऊ   ऊ   ऊ   ऊ   ऊ   ऊ

ऊ   ऊ   ऊ   ऊ   ऊ   ऊ

Name: _____   **Date**: _____

उ   ऊ   उ   ऊ   उ   ऊ

उ   ऊ   उ   ऊ   उ   ऊ

Lesson 4 – चतुर्थः पाठः

In this lesson, you will learn the next two vowels. Hope you have already practiced writing the first six vowels अ, आ, इ, ई, उ, and ऊ. {**Do not forget:** Learning is cumulative. Whatever you have learned in the previous class is important for further progression}.

 Writing

Sanskrit Alphabet	Transliteration	Pronunciation Guide
ऋ	Ru	Somewhere between <u>Ri</u> an <u>Ru</u> and the nearest is <u>Riu</u>
ॠ	RU	Long form of Riu

Remember: Not all sounds have an exact English equivalent. These two vowels fall in this category. But in Sanskrit, we have significant use for them. **Example:** The word for 'Saint' is ऋषिः (**Ru**shiH). Both these vowels have complex writing pattern. First practice with a *Guru*.

 अमृतभाषणम्‌ – amRutabhAShaNam – Spoken Exercises

Did you say 'hariH Om' or 'namaste' to greet anyone? Remember, with these words, you can greet anyone. Now we will teach you how to introduce your parents to other friends. For example, I want to say to my friends, "My father is Srinivas". Let us see how we do that.

Exercise 1: How do you say "My father is_____"

1. मम पिता _____ । (mama pitA _____ .)

Exercise 2: How do you say "My mother is_____"

1. मम माता _____ । (mama mAtA _____ .)

शब्दकोशः - shabdakoshaH - Vocabulary Words

 शुकः (shukaH)

 पिकः (pikaH)

 काकः (kAkaH)

 बकः (bakaH)

1. Follow the rhyme from the teacher and memorize the words and their meanings.

2. **Exercise:** Make up your own tune, using the words above.

भारतीयसंस्कृतिः – Indian Culture

In this lesson, your teacher will teach you about the Hindu Goddess "*pArvatI*". Complete the

activities following your teacher's suggestions.

Name: _____   **Date**: _____

ऋट   ऋट   ऋट   ऋट   ऋट   ऋट

ऋट   ऋट   ऋट   ऋट   ऋट   ऋट

Name: _____   **Date**: _____

ॠ   ॠ   ॠ   ॠ   ॠ   ॠ

ॠ   ॠ   ॠ   ॠ   ॠ   ॠ

Name: _____   Date: _____

ऋ   ऋ   ऋ   ऋ   ऋ   ऋ

ऋ   ऋ   ऋ   ऋ   ऋ   ऋ

Lesson 5 – पञ्चमः पाठः

Review all the vowels you have learnt from previous lessons. All the vowels leant until now, have a short and long form (अ, आ). In this lesson, you will be learning two more vowels. They are both long vowels. They do not have a corresponding short vowel. Pronunciation is the key in Sanskrit. If you are able to pronounce the entire alphabet clearly, you can easily master the language. Say it out loud when you are writing the alphabet.

 Writing

Sanskrit Alphabet	Transliteration	Pronunciation Guide
ए	e	ate
ऐ	ai	eye or sight

These vowels are both long and take two units of time to pronounce. Observe, the first vowel अ takes one unit of time, compared to the time taken by the second vowel आ, which takes two units of time. Take your time to practice well.

 अमृतभाषणम् – amRutabhAShaNam – Spoken Exercises

In the previous lesson, you have learned how to introduce your parents to friends. Now let's learn to introduce brother or sister.

Exercise 1: How do you say "My brother is _____."

1. मम भ्राता _____ । (mama bhrAtA _____ .)

Fill in the blank with your brother's name. Example:

मम भ्राता बलरामः। (mama bhrAtA balarAmaH)

Exercise 2: How do you say "My sister is _____."

1. मम भगिनी _____ । (mama bhaginI _____ .)

Fill in the blank with your sister's name. Example:

मम भगिनी अनूराधा । (mama bhaginI anUrAdhA)

शब्दकोशः - shabdakoshaH - Vocabulary Words

काश्मीरफलम् (kAshmIraphalam)

नारङ्गम् (nArangam)

कदलीफलम् (kadalIphalam)

द्राक्षाफलम् (drAkShAphalam)

1. Follow the rhyme from the teacher and memorize the words and their meanings.

2. **Exercise:** Make up your own tune, using the words above.

3. **Exercise:** Review all the vocabulary words learned in the previous lessons.

भारतीयसंस्कृतिः – Indian Culture

In this lesson, your teacher will teach you about the Hindu Goddess "*sarasvatI*". Complete the activities following your teacher's suggestions. Remember, you have learned a prayer shloka on goddess sarasvatI. Can you recall the prayer shloka on goddess **sarasvatI** ?

Name: _____   **Date:** _____

Name: _____   Date: _____

ऐ   ऐ   ऐ   ऐ   ऐ   ऐ

ऐ   ऐ   ऐ   ऐ   ऐ   ऐ

Name: _____   **Date:** _____

Lesson 6 – षष्ठमः पाठः

Did you practice all the vowels that you have learned so far? We will be learning two more long vowels in this lesson. Remember if अ takes one unit of time then आ takes two units of time. The time taken for the following vowels is two units of time.

 Writing

Sanskrit Alphabet	Transliteration	Pronunciation Guide
ओ	o	b<u>oa</u>t
औ	au	<u>ou</u>tdoor

Observe the minute difference between them in the script. First, work with the *Guru* and practice well in the worksheets following this lesson.

 अमृतभाषणम् – amRutabhAShaNam – Spoken Exercises

In the last few lessons, you have learned to introduce your father, mother, brother and sister. In this lesson, you will learn how to introduce your friend and guru. Let's see how we do that.

Exercise 1: How do you say "My friend is_____"

Fill in the blank with your friend's name. Example:

मम मित्रम् प्रदीपः ॥ (mama mitram pradIpaH)

1. मम मित्रम्_____ । (mama mitram _____ .)

Exercise 2: How do you say "My guru is_____"

1. मम गुरुः _____ । (mama guruH _____ .)

शब्दकोशः - shabdakoshaH - Vocabulary Words

 शिरः (shiraH - Head)

 केशः (keshaH - Hair)

 कर्णः (karNaH – Ear)

 नेत्रम् (netram – Eye)

1. Follow the rhyme from the teacher and memorize the words and their meanings.

2. **Exercise:** Make up your own tune, using the words above.

3. Recall the vocabulary words from the previous lessons.

भारतीयसंस्कृतिः – Indian Culture

In this lesson, your teacher will teach you about the Hindu God "*brahmA*" (pronounced as Bramha).

Complete the activities following your teacher's suggestions. "**brahmA**" is the great creator of life.

ओ ओ ओ ओ ओ ओ

ओ ओ ओ ओ ओ ओ

औ   औ   औ   औ   औ   औ

औ   औ   औ   औ   औ   औ

Name: _____   **Date:** _____

ओ औ ओ औ ओ औ

ओ औ ओ औ ओ औ

Lesson 7 – सप्तमः पाठः

Review all the vowels you have learnt so far. In this lesson, we will be learning the last two vowels. They both take one unit of time.

 Writing

Sanskrit Alphabet	Transliteration	Pronunciation Guide
अं	aM	Umm!
अः	aH	Uh!

These two vowels are called **anusvAra** and **visarga**. They occur widely in samskRutam.

 अमृतभाषणम् – amRutabhAShaNam – Spoken Exercises

In this lesson, we will learn how to ask someone their name. In English we say, "What is your name?" There is no gender specific question in English. But in Sanskrit, we will differentiate between genders. Let's see how we do this.

Exercise 1: How do we say "What is your name? (To male person)"

भवतः नाम किम् ? (bhavataH nAma kim ?)

You already know the answer to this question. (**Hint**: mama nAma _____)

Exercise 2: How do we say "What is your name? (To female person)"

भवत्याः नाम किम् ? (bhavatyAH nAma kim ?)

You already know the answer to this question too. (**Hint**: mama nAma _____)

When responding to the questions above, we do not differentiate the genders. Just the question word changes for male or female.

शब्दकोशः - shabdakoshaH - Vocabulary Words

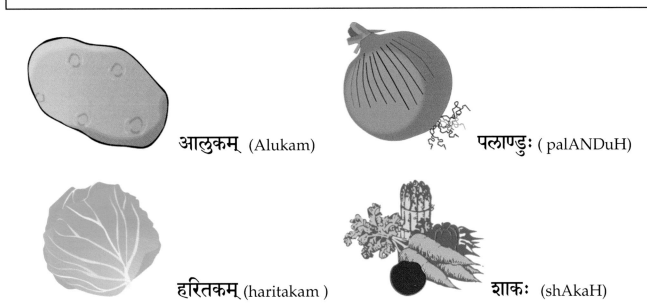

आलुकम् (Alukam)

पलाण्डुः (palANDuH)

हरितकम् (haritakam)

शाकः (shAkaH)

1. Follow the rhyme from the teacher and memorize the words and their meanings.

2. **Exercise:** Make up your own tune, using the words above.

3. Can you recall the rhyme for the fruits?

भारतीयसंस्कृतिः – Indian Culture

In this lesson your teacher will teach you about the Hindu God "*lakShmI*". Complete the activities following your teacher's suggestions.

Name: _____   **Date:** _____

अं अं अं अं अं अं अं

अं अं अं अं अं अं अं

Name: _____   **Date:** _____

अः   अः   अः   अः   अः   अः

अः   अः   अः   अः   अः   अः

Name: _____   **Date:** _____

अं   अः   अं   अः   अं   अः

_____
- -
_____

_____
- -
_____

_____
- -
_____

अं   अः   अं   अः   अं   अः

_____
- -
_____

_____
- -
_____

_____
- -
_____

Lesson 8 – अष्टमः पाठः

In the previous lesson we completed learning all vowels. In your K-Group level, you will be learning just the vowels. In this lesson, we will be reviewing all the vowels that you have learnt earlier.

 Writing

samskRutam vowels:

अ आ इ ई उ ऊ ऋ

ॠ ए ऐ ओ औ अं अः

Learn both devanAgari script and transliteration scheme. Vowels are pronounced clearly by opening your mouth. Do not use tongue, palate, teeth, or lips. Sounds should come from your throat and should be pronounced loud and clear. Always pronounce aloud while writing. Did your teacher teach you the alphabet rhyme? Isn't it easy to memorize the alphabet with a rhyme? Do you have any other creative ways to memorize them? Can you create a rhyme with a different tune? Do not hesitate. Try it out.

 अमृतभाषणम् – amRutabhAShaNam – Spoken Exercises

By this time you might have understood, **मम** (mama) means "my". It is a small but powerful word. You can introduce whatever belongs to you with 'mama'. Let's see how we do that.

Let's learn how to say "my head", or "my ear". **Remember the magic word:** मम (mama) means "my". **(Point with your finger, while you tell)**

Exercise 1: How do you say "My head"?   मम शिरः।   (mama shiraH ।)

Exercise 2: How do you say "My ear"?   मम कर्णः ।   (mama karNaH ।)

शब्दकोशः - shabdakoshaH - Vocabulary Words

This week, you will review the vocabulary words that you have learned in the previous lessons.

Exercise 1: Look at the words below and recall their meaning. (Hint: Recall your vocab rhyme).

शशः (shashaH), शुकः (shukaH), नारङ्गम् (nArangam), काकः (kAkaH), कदलीफलम्

(kadalIphalam), नेत्रम् (netram), पलाण्डुः (palANDuH), गजः (gajaH)

Exercise 2: Look at the pictures below and recall the Sanskrit words for them. (Hint: Recall your vocab rhyme).

भारतीयसंस्कृतिः – Indian Culture

In this lesson, your teacher will teach you about the Hindu God "*viShNu*". Complete the activities

following your teacher's suggestions.

Name: _____   **Date**: _____

अ आ इ ई उ ऊ ऋ

ॠ ए ऐ ओ औ अं अः

Name: _____   **Date:** _____

अ आ इ ई उ ऊ ऋ

ॠ ए ऐ ओ औ अं अः

Name: _____   **Date:** _____

अ इ उ ऋ आ ई ऊ

ए ओ ऋ अं ऐ ओ अः

Lesson 9 – नवमः पाठः

We have completed learning all the vowels. In this level, you will be learning just the vowels. Now let's review all the vowels that you have learned.

samskRutam vowels:

अ आ इ ई उ ऊ ऋ

ॠ ए ऐ ओ औ अं अः

Learn both devanAgari script and transliteration scheme. Vowels are pronounced clearly by opening your mouth. Do not use tongue, palate, teeth, or lips. Sounds should come from your throat and should be pronounced loud and clear. Always say it out loud while writing.

 अमृतभाषणम् – amRutabhAShaNam – Spoken Exercises

Let's review: मम (mama) means "my". Remember, you can introduce whatever belongs to you with 'mama'. As you have seen in the previous lesson, how to tell "my ear", "my eye" etc.

You can use this to tell even "my elephant" etc. for animals and birds.

Exercise 1: How do you say "My elephant" => मम गजः । (mama gajaH ।) (Point to your elephant toy or picture, while you tell)

Exercise 2: How do you say "My parrot" => मम शुकः । (mama shukaH.)

शब्दकोशः - shabdakoshaH - Vocabulary Words

Exercise: Pictures have been associated with wrong words. Identify and correct them.

	आलुकम् (Alukam)		शिरः (shiraH)
	काकः (kAkaH)		एकादश (ekAdasha)
	द्वे (dve)		गजः (gajaH)
	काश्मीरफलम् (kAshmIraphalam)		पिकः (pikaH)

भारतीयसंस्कृतिः – Indian Culture

In this lesson your teacher will teach you about Hindu Gods "*rAma*" and "*sItA*". Complete the activities following your teacher's suggestions. Do you remember the "*rAma*" shabda chanting?

Name: _____   **Date:** _____

उ ऊ अ आ अं अः

ओ औ ऋ ॠ ए ऐ इ ई

Name: _____   **Date:** _____

इ ई ॠ ॠ ए ऐ

अ अं अः आ ओ औ

Name: _____ **Date:** _____

उ अ ऊ आ ओ औ

ए इ ऐ ओ उ ई ऋ ॠ

Lesson 10 – दशमः पाठः

In this lesson, we will review all the vowels and their corresponding transliteration scheme that you have learned.

 Writing

samskRutam vowels:

अ a   आ A   इ i   ई I   उ u   ऊ U

ऋ Ru   ॠ RU   ए e   ऐ ai   ओ o

औ au   अं aM   अः aH

Learn both *devanAgari* script and *transliteration* scheme. Vowels are pronounced clearly by opening your mouth. Sounds should come from your throat and should be pronounced loud and clear. Always say it out loud while writing.

 अमृतभाषणम् – amRutabhAShaNam – Spoken Exercises

Review all the spoken exercises from the previous lessons. In the last few lessons, you have learned how to say "my elephant", "my bird", "my ear" etc. You can use 'mama' with fruits.

Once you learn a vocabulary word for any item that belongs to you, you can use 'mama' with that. Let us see how we do that.

Exercise 1: How do you say "My orange fruit"? मम नारङ्गम् । (mama nAra~gam.

Pronounce as nArangam.)

Exercise 2: How do you say "My apple"? मम काश्मीरफलम् । (mama

kAshmIraphalam .)

शब्दकोशः - shabdakoshaH - Vocabulary Words

Review all of the vocabulary words that you have learned from the previous lessons.

Exercise: Match the pictures in column 1 with the Sanskrit words in the column 2

	पिकः (pikaH)
	गजः (gajaH)
	हरितकम् (haritakam)
	नारङ्गम् (nArangam)
	केशः (keshaH)

भारतीयसंस्कृतिः – Indian Culture

In this lesson, your teacher will teach you about the Hindu God "*hanumAn*". Complete the activities

following your teacher's suggestions.

Name: _____   **Date:** _____

अ आ इ ई उ ऊ ऋ ॠ

ए ऐ ओ औ अं अः

Name: _____   **Date:** _____

a A i I u U Ru

RU e ai o au aM aH

Name: _____   **Date**: _____

ए ॠ अं इ उ ओ

ऐ अः औ ऊ ॠ ई

"श्रृगालस्य कथा "– एकः गानीयः – "Story of Fox" – A musical (Short Version)

कथका / कथकः : एकः एकः श्रृगालः । एकः एकः श्रृगालः ।

छात्राः : श्रृगालस्य नाम किम् ?

कथका : श्रृगालस्य नाम लघुपादः ।

छात्राः : एकः एकः श्रृगालः । एकः एकः श्रृगालः ।

कथका : बुभुक्षा पीडितः । पिपासा पीडितः । श्रृगालः बुभुक्षा पीडितः वा?

छात्राः : आम् श्रृगालः बुभुक्षा पीडितः ।

कथका : श्रृगालः पिपासा पीडितः वा?

छात्राः : आम् श्रृगालः पिपासा पीडितः ।

छात्राः : ओ ! ...अद्य श्रृगालः किं करोति ?

कथका : वनं गच्छति श्रृगालः, श्रृगालः, श्रृगालः। श्रृगालः कुत्र गच्छति ?

छात्राः : श्रृगालः वनं गच्छति । वने किमपि पश्यति वा?

कथका : आम् , श्रृगालः द्राक्षाफलं पश्यति ।

छात्राः : यम् , यम् ..... द्राक्षाफलम् ।

कथका : उपरि उपरि लतायां द्राक्षाफलं पश्यति । उपरि उपरि लतायां द्राक्षाफलं पश्यति ।

छात्राः : श्रृगालः द्राक्षाफलं खादति वा ?

कथका : कथां श्रृणोतु । उपरि उपरि लतायां द्राक्षाफलं पश्यति ।

एकवारम् उत्पतति । फलं न लभते । द्विवारम् उत्पतति । फलं न लभते ।

त्रिवारम् उत्पतति । फलं न लभते । पुनः पुनः उत्पतति । फलं न लभते ।

श्रृगालः चिन्तयति । आम्लं द्राक्षाफलं । अहं न इच्छामि । आम्लं द्राक्षाफलं । अहं न इच्छामि ।

इति उक्त्वा श्रृगालः गृहं गच्छति ।

See Note Below[2]

"SRugAlasya kathA" – "Story of Fox"–A musical (Short Version)

kathakA/ kathakaH : ekaH ekaH shRugAlaH | ekaH ekaH shRugAlaH |

ChAtrAH : shRugAlasya nAma kim ?

kathakA : shRugAlasya nAma laghuupAdaH |

ChAtrAH: ekaH ekaH shRugAlaH | ekaH ekaH shRugAlaH |

kathakA: bubhukShA pIDitaH | pipAsA pIDitaH | shRugAlaH bubhukShA pIDitaH vA?

ChAtrAH: Am shRugAlaH bubhukShA pIDitaH |

kathakA: shRugAlaH pipAsA pIDitaH vA?

ChAtrAH : Am shRugAlaH pipAsA   pIDitaH |

ChAtrAH: o !...adya shRugAlaH kiM   karoti ?

kathakA: vanaM gacChati shRugAlaH, shRugAlaH, shRugAlaH| shRugAlaH kutra gacChati ?

ChAtrAH: shRugAlaH vanaM gacChati | vane kimapi pashyati vA?

kathakA: Am shRugAlaH drAkShAphalaM pashyati |

ChAtrAH: yam, yam..... drAkShAphalam |

kathakA: upari upari latAyAM drAkShAphalaM pashyati | upari upari latAyAM drAkShAphalaM pashyati |

ChAtrAH: shRugAlaH drAkShAphalaM khAdati vA ?

kathakA: kathAM shruNotu | upari upari latAyAM drAkShAphalaM pashyati | ekavAram utpatati | phalaM na labhate |

dvivAram   utpatati | phalaM na labhate |

trivAram   utpatati | phalaM   na labhate |

punaH punaH utpatati | phalaM na labhate |

shRugAlaH chintayati | AmlaM   drAkShAphalaM | ahaM na icChAmi |

AmlaM   drAkShAphalaM | aham na icChAmi |

iti uktvA shRugAlaH, gRuham gacChati |

See Note Below[4]

---

[3] This and other images in this book are from clickr.com

[4] This image is in the public domain because its copyright has expired. This applies to the United States, where works published prior to 1978 were copyright protected for a maximum of 75 years. Works published before 1923, in this case 1851, are now in the public domain.

Summary

In this level, you have learned how to write vowels in **devanAgarI** and their corresponding transliteration in English. Transliteration is taught so early in the learning process to help children quickly pick-up writing, and reading. This covers the learning areas of **paThanam** (reading) and **lekhanam** (writing). The prayer shlokAs, mangaLa shloka, shAnti mantras, shabda chanting, and vocabulary rhymes will cover **shravaNam** (listening) and **mananam** (chanting, memorizing and pattern recognition in the mind etc.,). "amRutabhAShaNam" section together with vocabulary words and "story musical" contribute to **bhAShaNam** (speaking, conversing and collaborating skills). Especially, chanting brings peace, creating a positive energy in the mind and contributes to the overall well-being of the learner.

Course Evaluation

This book can be adopted for a course spanning 4-6 months consisting of at least 10 weekend classes for the children of ages 3-6 years or an absolute beginner of any age. This course can be evaluated for awarding a K-Group (skanda-gaNapatI) Level certificate based on the following:

- Attendance – Out of 10 contact classes at least 8 must be attended. The remaining two missing classes should be made up with teacher or supporting volunteer.
- Participation in the class.
- Daily quiz (not more than 5 minutes)
- Books, Notebooks and Binder Checks
- Assignments/ Homeworks
- Class/ curriculum activities like drawing, painting, coloring covering the creative areas.
- Final Examination can be conducted for Verbal and Written skills– Verbal test includes pronunciation, chanting, speaking etc. and Written test includes writing in devanAgarI and transliteration.
- Final Project can be a poster, a collage, creating a flip-book, or performance of a story with props.

It is our sincere belief that, all the participants will enjoy learning Sanskrit in skanda-gaNapatI Level using this Simple Learning Series presentation.

॥ ॐ तत् सत् ॥